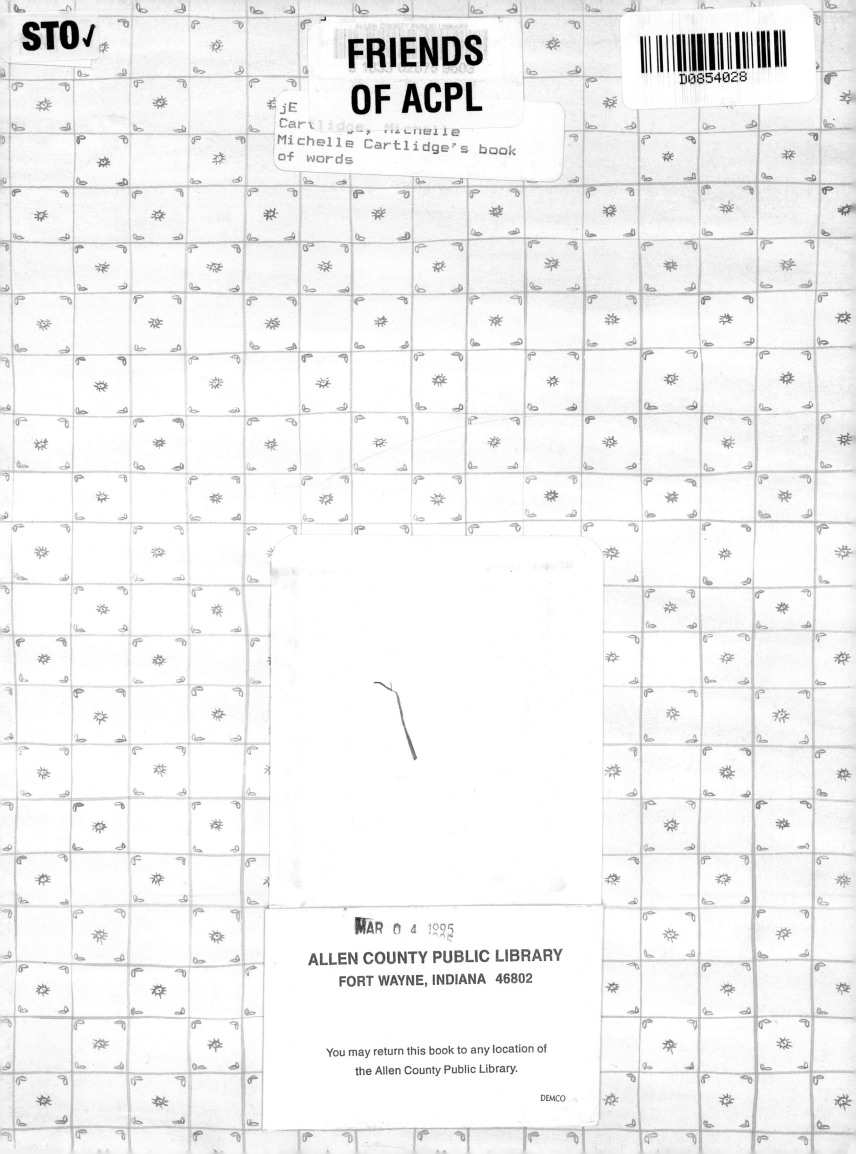

To Stefan

·ᏀᎧ·ᏀᎧ·ᏀᎧ·ᏀᎧ·ᏀᎧ·ᏀᎧ·ᏀᎧ·ᏀᎧ·ᏀᎧ·ᏀᎧ·ᏀᎧ·ᏀᎧ·ᏀᎧ·ᏀᎧ·ᏀᎧ·ᏀᎧ·

Copyright © 1994 by Michelle Cartlidge
All rights reserved.

CIP Data is available.

Published in the United States 1994
by Dutton Children's Books, a division of Penguin Books USA Inc.
375 Hudson Street, New York, New York 10014
Designed by Adrian Leichter
Printed in Hong Kong
First Edition
1 3 5 7 9 10 8 6 4 2
ISBN 0-525-45254-0

Michelle Cartlidge's
BOOK OF
WORDS

DUTTON CHILDREN'S BOOKS · NEW YORK

THE MOUSES' HOUSE

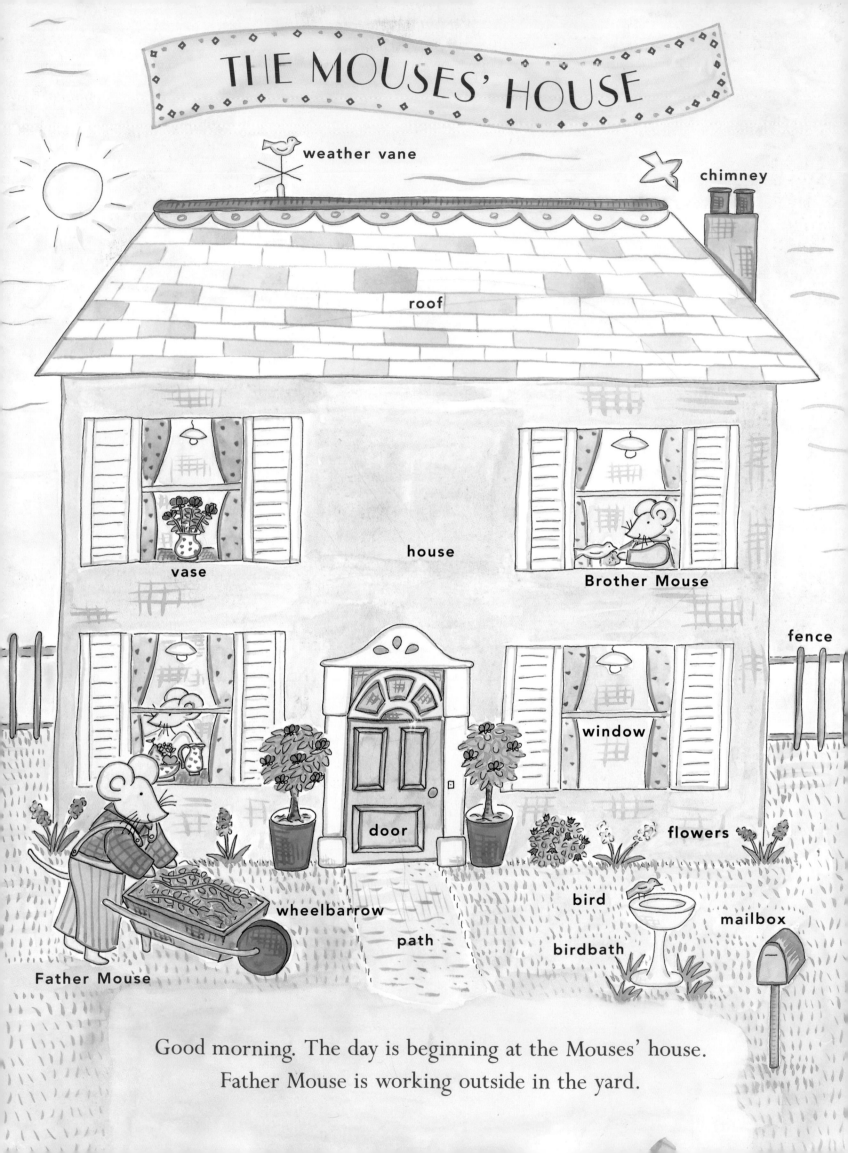

weather vane

chimney

roof

house

vase

Brother Mouse

fence

window

door

flowers

wheelbarrow

bird

mailbox

path

birdbath

Father Mouse

Good morning. The day is beginning at the Mouses' house.
Father Mouse is working outside in the yard.

sky

bird

sun

mobile

toys   playroom

bedroom

bunk beds

Sister Mouse   cradle   Baby Mouse

mirror   window

chair   bed

Brother Mouse   bedroom

toilet   sink

bath-tub

bathroom   hall

kitchen

Mother Mouse   hall

lamp   couch

chair

living room

table

grass

frog

Mother Mouse is making breakfast in the kitchen. Sister Mouse is looking after Baby Mouse. Where is Brother Mouse?

IN THE BATHROOM

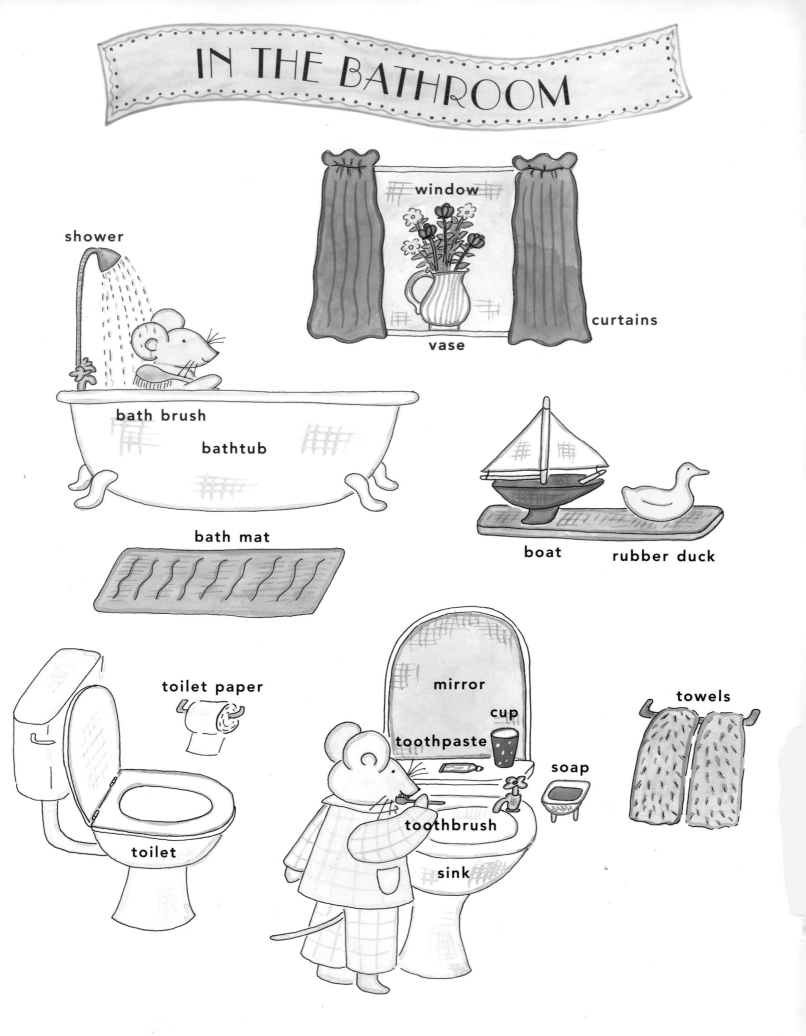

shower

window

vase

curtains

bath brush

bathtub

boat

rubber duck

bath mat

toilet paper

mirror

cup

toothpaste

soap

towels

toothbrush

toilet

sink

The young mice are in the bathroom. Brother Mouse
is brushing his teeth. Sister Mouse is taking a bath.

GETTING DRESSED

skirt

shirt

necklace

Sister Mouse

rattle

playsuit

bib

stretch suit

Baby Mouse

hat

overalls

cup

bottle

Brother Mouse

sweater

The mice are ready to get dressed.
What should they wear today?

THE BUS STOP

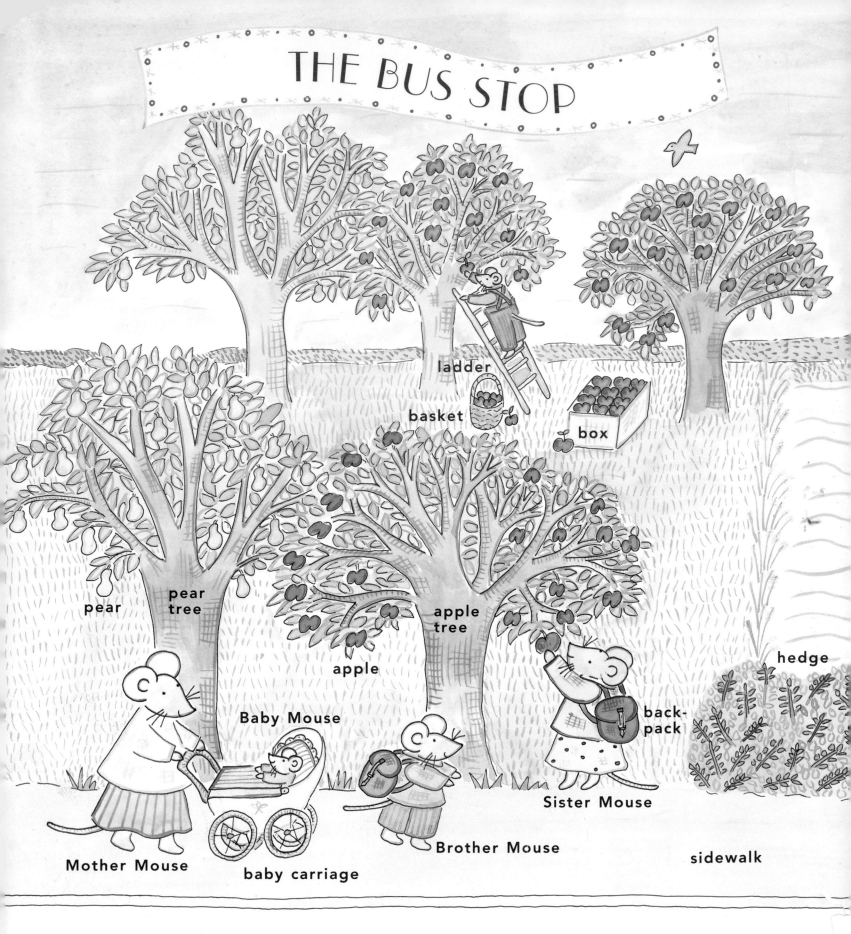

ladder

basket

box

pear pear tree

apple

apple tree

Baby Mouse

Mother Mouse

baby carriage

Brother Mouse

Sister Mouse

back-pack

hedge

sidewalk

Mother Mouse walks the Mouse children to the bus stop.
Sister Mouse picks an apple for the teacher.

The bus driver waits for Brother and Sister Mouse.
Off they go to school.

AT SCHOOL

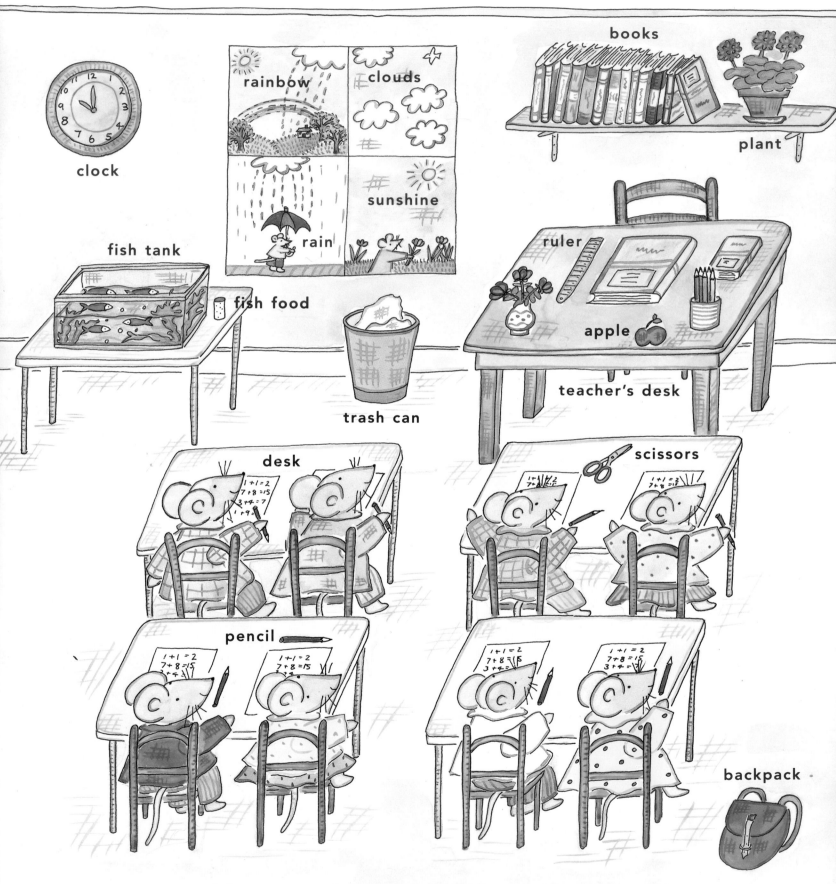

clock

rainbow

clouds

books

plant

fish tank

fish food

sunshine

rain

ruler

apple

teacher's desk

trash can

desk

scissors

pencil

backpack

The Mouse children come to school to learn.
Brother and Sister Mouse are in the same class.

alphabet

A B C D E F G H I J K L M N O P Q R S T U V W X Y Z

$1 + 1 = 2$
$7 + 8 = 15$
$3 + 4 = 7$
$1 + 9 = 10$

numbers

chalkboard

light

globe

chalk

eraser

teacher

colored pencils

paper

principal

Pay attention, young mice.
The teacher is talking.

SHOPPING IN TOWN

Hotel

Library

tree

Candy Store

Bakery

Grocery Store

door

garbage can

sidewalk

Mouse family

delivery boy

grocer

bike

The Mouse family goes shopping in town.
The street is busy.

Post Office

Office Building

Restaurant

Toy Store

awning

diners

street-lamp

taxi

passenger

crosswalk

AT THE CANDY STORE

The candy store is full of wonderful things.
Brother and Sister Mouse choose chocolate fudge.

AT THE BAKERY

mixing bowl

sugar

baker

bread

cookies

oven

butter

wooden spoon

knife

rolling pin

oven mitts

apron

French bread

counter

cupcakes

doughnuts   croissants

cookies

Mother Mouse buys a loaf of bread at the bakery.
The smell of freshly baked cookies fills the air.

AT THE GROCERY STORE

cereal boxes

cookies · jams · pickles

bottles

paper towels

fish

carrots · mushrooms

peppers

scale

crabs

shrimp

fish

seafood counter

The next stop is the grocery store. Sister Mouse is putting
a pineapple in the shopping cart.

Brother Mouse has knocked over a pile of oranges.
Oops! He has to pick them up.

IN THE GARDEN

fence

tree

basket

carrots

strawberries

tulips

irises

garbage can

wheelbarrow

Father Mouse loves to work in the garden.
He grows flowers and vegetables.

bushes

bird

pots

fork

shed

garden hose

watering can

pail

shovel

compost heap

trowel

sunflowers

lettuce

rake

tomatoes

seedlings

bouquet

roses

seed
packets

flower beds

daffodils

Brother Mouse likes sunflowers.
What flowers do you like?

IN THE KITCHEN

spice rack

teacups

picture

curtains

windowsill

Baby Mouse

spoons

plates

dishwashing soap

freezer

refrigerator

flour

sink

scale

pots

stove

bow

high chair

cupcakes

Sister Mouse

chair

Mother Mouse

Something good is cooking. The Mouse family is making
cupcakes. Mother Mouse stirs the frosting in a pot.

window

bird

flower-pots

teapot

coffeepot

creamer

canisters

bowls

blender

casserole

paper cups

mixer

frying pan

sauce-pan

onions

fruit bowl

bread

knife

drawer

mixing bowl

apron

table

milk bottle

cabinet

Father Mouse

Brother Mouse

Father Mouse mixes the batter in a bowl.
Here comes Brother Mouse with the milk.

AT THE PLAYGROUND

tree

flowers

swings

ball

slide

climbing bars

The Mouse children love the playground. Some mice are
on the slide. Be careful on that swing, Brother Mouse!

FAVORITE TOYS

stuffed rabbit

doll

toy truck

ball

toy car

mobile

kite

rocking horse

giraffe   bear   duck   fish

teddy bears

skateboard

colored pencils

top

puzzle

blocks

The Mouse children keep their toys in the playroom.
What is your favorite toy?

A BIRTHDAY PARTY

pin-the-tail-on-the-donkey

lamp

picture

presents

bureau

candles

chair

plates

cups

cake

cupcakes

sandwiches

punch

tablecloth

Mother Mouse

It is Brother Mouse's birthday. His friends have come
to his party. There are presents to open and games to play.

bows

streamers

window

balloons

curtains

cards

chair

pillow

hat

Sister Mouse

Father Mouse

table

book

games

toy train

friends

Brother Mouse

Soon everyone will eat sandwiches, cake, and ice cream.
How many candles are on the cake?

BEDTIME

stars

moon

curtains

window

clock

books

bookshelf

sheets

blanket

bunk beds

ladder

book

cradle

pillow

rug

lamp

night-stand

It is bedtime. Father Mouse is reading one last story.
Then good night, Mouse children.